MEET THE COMMUNITY HELPERS!

A DAY WITH A TEACHER

by Mari Schuh
illustrated by Dean Gray

Ideas for Parents & Teachers

Grasshopper Books introduce children to fiction at the earliest levels. Fun storylines and easy-to-follow text support early readers as they learn to read informational fiction and enhance their imagination. Sight words, repetitive sentence patterns, and fun illustrations support early readers.

Before Reading

- Discuss the cover illustration. What do they see?
- Look at the picture glossary together. Discuss the words.

Read the Book

- Read the book to the child, or have him or her read independently.
- "Walk" through the book and look at the illustrations. Who is the main character? What is happening in the story?

After Reading

- Prompt the child to think more. Ask: Would you like to be a teacher? Why or why not?

Grasshopper Books are published by Jump!
5357 Penn Avenue South
Minneapolis, MN 55419
www.jumplibrary.com

Library of Congress Cataloging-in-Publication Data

Names: Schuh, Mari C., 1975– author.
Gray, Dean, illustrator.
Title: A day with a teacher / by Mari Schuh;
[illustrated by Dean Gray].
Description: Minneapolis, MN: Jump!, Inc., 2025.
Series: Meet the community helpers! | Includes index.
Audience: Ages 5–8
Identifiers: LCCN 2023049876 (print)
LCCN 2023049877 (ebook)
ISBN 9798892130981 (hardcover)
ISBN 9798892130998 (paperback)
ISBN 9798892131001 (ebook)
Subjects: LCSH: Readers (Primary)
Teachers—Juvenile fiction. | LCGFT: Readers
(Publications).
Classification: LCC PE1119.2 .S37296 2025 (print)
LCC PE1119.2 (ebook)
DDC 428.6/2—dc23/eng/20231124
LC record available at https://lccn.loc.gov/2023049876
LC ebook record available at https://lccn.loc.gov/2023049877

Editor: Jenna Gleisner
Direction and Layout: Emma Almgren-Bersie
Illustrator: Dean Gray

Printed in the United States of America at
Corporate Graphics in North Mankato, Minnesota.

Table of Contents

Teaching Students

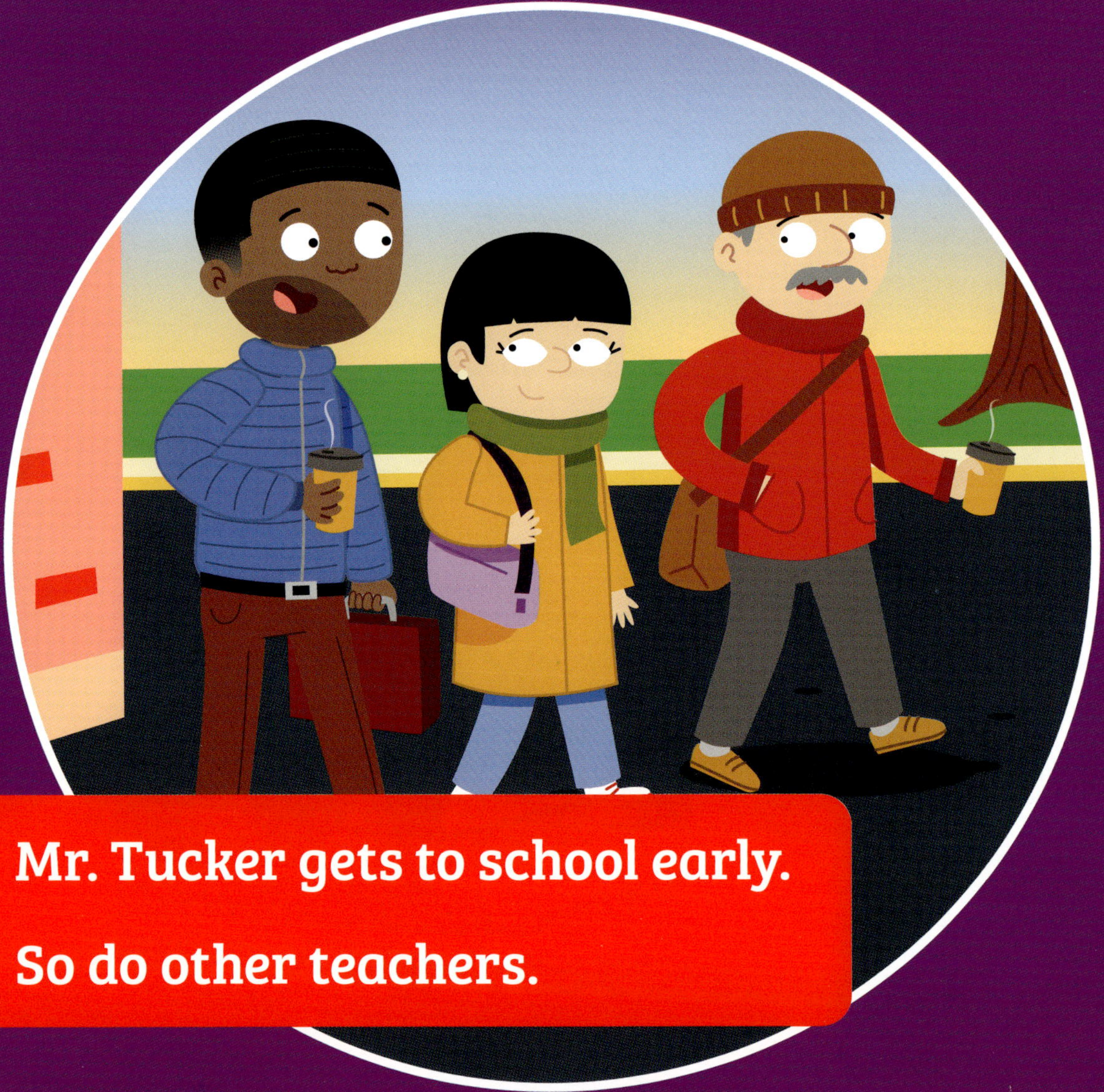

Mr. Tucker gets to school early.

So do other teachers.

He gets his classroom ready.

He greets his students
at the door.

“Good morning!” he says.

"I hope you all studied your words!" says Mr. Tucker. "We will start with a spelling quiz."

“The first word is *apple*. Please spell *apple* for number one,” says Mr. Tucker.

After spelling, it is time for math.

"Who can tell me if 6 is an even or odd number?" asks Mr. Tucker.

He calls on Dee to answer.

"Even!" says Dee.

"Correct! Nice job," says Mr. Tucker.

4 5 6 7 8 9 1

After lessons, it is time for lunch.
The students eat in the cafeteria.

Mr. Tucker eats with the other teachers.

He also grades the spelling quizzes.

Recess is after lunch.

Today, it is Mr. Tucker's turn to supervise.

He watches over the playground.

He sees that Dee looks sad.

He asks what is wrong.

They talk it out together.

Art is the last lesson of the day.

Mr. Tucker helps the students mix paints.

"Good job, everyone! Tomorrow, we will learn how plants grow!" he says.

After school, Mr. Tucker goes home.

He writes lesson plans.

He gets ready to teach tomorrow!

Quiz Time!

What did Mr. Tucker do after school?

A. read a book **B.** wrote lesson plans
C. graded the spelling quizzes **D.** played a game

Teacher Tools

Take a look at some of a teacher's tools!

desk

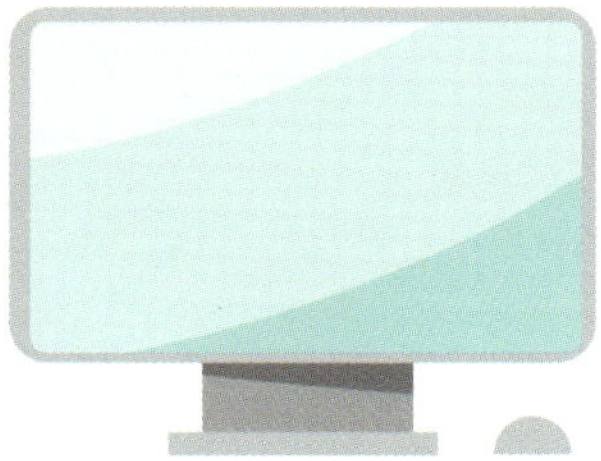

computer

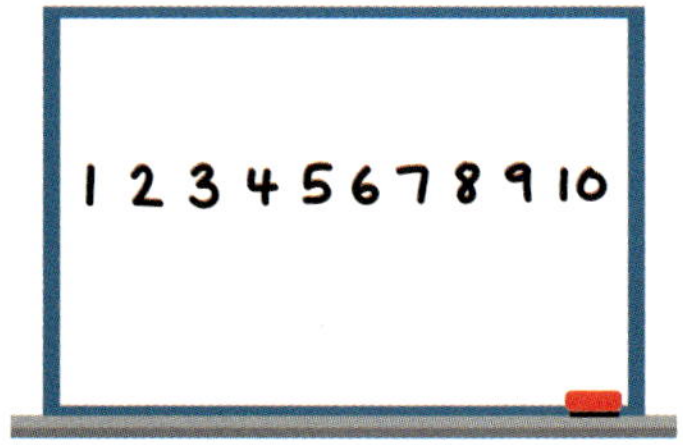

whiteboard

books

pencils

Quiz Time! Answer Key: **B.** wrote lesson plans

Picture Glossary

cafeteria
A room in a school where meals are served and eaten.

greets
Welcomes.

lesson plans
Lists of steps and activities a teacher will teach.

quiz
A short test to find out what students have learned.

students
People who study at a school.

supervise
To watch over.

Index

To Learn More

FACT SURFER

Finding more information is as easy as 1, 2, 3.

1. Go to www.factsurfer.com
2. Enter "**adaywithateacher**" into the search box.
3. Choose your book to see a list of websites.